...dwset,
Injoy! Joanne
x

To the Bakery & Beyond

Recipes and reflections on real food free from sugar and gluten

Jo Dance

Published in 2016 by Joy Food Revolution
www.joyfoodrevolution.com

ISBN 978-1-78132-521-6

British Library Cataloguing in Publication Data
A CIP catalogue record for this book is available from the British Library

Printed on responsibly sourced paper

Notes for the Reader
The times given are an approximate guide only. Preparation times differ according to the techniques used by different people, and cooking times may also vary from those given. Optional ingredients, variations or serving suggestions have not been included in the calculations.

Contents

 = Grain Free   = Vegan   = Vegan Option

Thank You

My heartfelt thanks goes out to all those who have been an inspiration to me in making this book.

To Kirsten Chick, a wonderful nutritionist who teaches me so much.

To Steven Acuff and Rani Louise for sharing with me their knowledge and support so kindly, and to all the other local nutritionists (sorry you are too many to name) who have given their thoughts and helped me along the way.

To Chris Dance for the wonderful pictures and design, and to all my friends and family for being my patient and kind tasting panel!

Introduction

I've always had an interest in nutrition, and have become increasingly fascinated with my mission finding and creating food that is delicious, while beneficial for my body. I'm passionate about health and wellbeing, and I've found myself on a lifelong journey to discover how to use food as medicine.

This book was born of my frustration in not being able to buy decent snacks and treats for my son without refined sugar and gluten. I would often get asked for recipes after sharing my food with friends and family, and most of them were on scraps of paper in my illegible writing, so I decided to put them all into a small booklet. A few years and grey hairs later it has finally come together into this little book.

I've been curious about holistic health since I was a child, when I suffered from bad eczema. After getting through lots of steroid cream to no avail, I went to see a naturopath who treated me with various herbs and hydrotherapy, and it all cleared up in a few weeks. Since my twenties, I've had an interest in naturopathic nutrition, macrobiotics, and more recently Chinese Medicine.

The recipes I came up with in this book are all ones I've adapted or invented. Where possible I've included both cup and gram measures, but unfortunately on some of the recipes this just wasn't possible. I find my digital scales invaluable! Things evolve and develop fast in the world of food and nutrition. There are new techniques and research coming out all the time, as well as the uncovering of old and traditional gems of knowledge.

I hope you enjoy it!

Each individual's dietary needs are unique, and I would suggest seeking the advice of a good GP, nutritionist, or acupuncturist for any specific health conditions or allergies.

Mindful Eating

"When walking, walk. When eating, eat."

Zen Proverb

If you are eating while overloaded with stimuli and under stress, your body doesn't know that it's supposed to be digesting. Paying attention while eating assures full digestion as well as full nutritional benefit. Eating slowly is also crucial for good health, ideally chewing each mouthful at least 30 times (it's not quite as long as it sounds!). If or when you have the time, one practice to help with this is putting your fork down in between each mouthful.

When you take time to experience your food through all your senses – taste, smell, sight, sound of surroundings, and touch (the movement of utensils and the feel of the food) – you are likely to be truly nourished.

"Eating mindfully is a most important practice of meditation. We can eat in a way that we restore the cookie of our childhood. The present moment is filled with joy and happiness. If you are attentive, you will see it."

Thich Nhat Hanh

Sugar Musings

So why does refined sugar get such a bad press? Well, the old adage, "You are what you eat" should really be replaced with, "You are what your body does with what you eat". I think the simplistic "calories in and calories out" argument is now very out of date. What is far more useful is to consider how energy is stored in our bodies. In terms of refined sugar (which I'll generally just refer to as "sugar"), it does a good deal of harm to our bodies when consumed regularly.

Sugar is an addictive, toxic substance. Our ancestors didn't have any sugar, and our systems haven't adapted to it. Sugar suppresses the hormone leptin, which tells your body when to stop eating, and so you want more. It makes us acidic, draws out minerals from our body, destroys B vitamins, and harms the liver. It spikes our insulin levels, which means that more energy is stored as fat, and makes us more tired and likely to eat in an effort to compensate.

My recipes contain higher levels of protein than most traditional sweet foods, and alongside good fats in the forms of coconut oils and organic butter, these foods help to lessen the detrimental effects of the sweeteners. They do this by slowing down the release of sugar into the bloodstream, compared with conventional sugar-laden "treats". Because they contain rich food sources, it's harder to keep eating these more healthful counterparts in the way that one could quite easily get through a whole packet of biscuits.

What to Use Instead?

We are now finding out that many alternatives to sugar are just as bad, or, in the case of artificial sweeteners, even worse. Things also change fast: I used to use agave syrup before I stumbled across the fact that it's actually not much better than sugar, as it's high in fructose and is often very processed. Unfortunately, it's still used in many "health" products, along with high-fructose corn syrup, which is definitely one to avoid.

For health reasons, the main sweetener I use is brown rice syrup[1]. Rice syrup is a mild sweetener and therefore a more healthful choice. However, larger amounts will also lead to a rise in blood sugar and insulin levels and so would take some of that benefit away. Barley malt can be used as an alternative.

Some people think honey[2] is OK to use. It is a highly nutritious food, containing many minerals, enzymes, and antioxidants. Others suggest avoiding it, mainly because of its high fructose content and the fact that most honeys out there have been highly processed and pasteurised. This destroys many of its valuable nutrients, and it removes most of the healthful pollen grains. So I'd recommend raw or unpasteurised honey. If you want to use honey instead of rice syrup, you can substitute the same quantity in all my recipes. However, honey is a lot sweeter than rice syrup, so ideally you would experiment with using less. Please steer clear of the cheap, nasty brands.

If you are used to the stronger sweet taste of sugar or other sweeteners, you might find my recipes don't taste sweet enough. Feel free to up the amount of sweetness used, but keep experimenting as your taste buds change and you will probably find you can gradually use less.

For health reasons, I think it's worth minimising the amount of sweet food we eat. If you're anything like me, that's not easy! The recipes in this book aren't meant for everyday consumption, and ideally we would have little or no sweet foods in our diets at all. For now, I'm compromising. My thoughts are, if you're going to have something sweet anyway, it's worth having something that's not putting your body under unnecessary stress.

1   Biona sell one that is widely available.
2   Sainsbury's sell a Wildflower honey by Littleover Apiary. Paynes Bee Farm and Raw Health are brands I really like.

Fabulous Fermentation

Many of my recipes containing flour suggest you leave them to rest before cooking. This allows for some fermentation to take place, making it easier for our bodies to digest. Traditional cultures have used this preparation technique for their grains, nuts, and seeds for centuries.

It has taken decades of research to get back to eating the way our great-great-grandparents did. We now know that the process of fermenting grains and beans before eating them neutralises phytic acid, and enzyme inhibitors, and breaks down gluten, sugars, and other difficult-to-digest elements. A diet high in unfermented whole grains can lead to mineral deficiencies and loss of bone density.

It may sound like a faff, but once you're in the habit it takes no time at all. Our kitchen usually has a bowl or two of something soaking sitting around.

For more on fermenting foods and traditional techniques there are some wonderful books out there such as *Wild Fermentation: The Flavour, Nutrition, and Craft of Live-Culture Foods* by Sandor Ellix Katz, and *Nourishing Traditions* by Sally Fallon, which has extensive notes on how to properly prepare grains, nuts and seeds. There are also some informative websites such as www.nourishedkitchen.com.

Soaking Nuts & Seeds

"The food you eat can either be the safest and most powerful form of medicine or the slowest form of poison."

Ann Wigmore

Soaking nuts, grains, and seeds removes most of the toxic substances found in them, such as phytic acid and tannins. These exist naturally so that the seed can survive until proper growing conditions are present, but they can be harmful if ingested.

To prepare, cover all these types of foods in plenty of warm water, and add a little lemon juice or unpasteurised apple cider vinegar. For **seeds**, add a pinch of salt to the bowl. Soak for 8 hours or more. Drain and rinse well before use.

Cashew nuts only require 3-6 hours soaking. **Rice and beans** benefit from 24 hours soaking.

Buckwheat needs dry roasting in a pan for a few minutes, then rinsing well before cooking. **Hemp seeds** are another exception and don't need soaking. I just roast them in a baking tray in a low oven for a few hours to bring out their lovely nutty flavour.

Unless you are using the **nuts and seeds** straight away, store them in the fridge in an airtight container for up to 3 days. Alternatively dehydrate them in a dehydrator, or oven set at 80°C for 6 hours or until completely dried out. They will then store like normal dried nuts.

"We must make organic the conventional choice and not the exception available only to the rich and educated."

Maria Rodale

Snacks & Biscuits

Carob Balls

Super quick and versatile, these yummy balls make a great sweet treat. The cinnamon in them helps to balance blood sugar levels.

PREPARATION **10 mins**   COOKING **None**   MAKES **16**

1 cup/160g	**pre-soaked dried fruit** choose from apricots, prunes or raisins[1]
1 ½ cups/150g	**ground almonds**
1 ½ cups/150g	**desiccated coconut**
¼ cup/40g	**coconut oil** – melted
1 cup/70g	**seeds** such as pumpkin, sunflower, sesame, and hemp or chai[2]
½ cup/50g	**carob powder**
2 tsp	**ground cinnamon**
2 tsp	**vanilla extract**
a little	**desiccated coconut, ground almonds and carob powder** for rolling

In a blender, whizz the seeds until fine.

Add in the drained dried fruit, melted coconut oil and vanilla extract, and mix until smooth.

Add in the ground almonds and mix again. The mixture will be quite moist but not too runny – add more ground almonds or desiccated coconut if it's too wet.

Shape into 3 cm balls, and roll in desiccated coconut, ground almonds or carob powder.

Store in the fridge.

1   Soak the fruit in lots of warm water, overnight if possible or for at least half an hour.
2   If you're using hemp or chai seeds, no more than ¼ cup.

Carob Balls freeze well too. If you're taking them out with you on a warm day, take them frozen so they'll keep for longer before going too soft. Get creative and add things like cardamom, bee pollen, maca, lacuma powder, or spirulina. Try replacing the carob with cacao powder and/or the coconut oil with cacao butter for a chocolatey treat! Ground brazil nuts or cashews could also be used in place of ground almonds.

Sesame Sticks

This is my version of Sesame Snaps, and these are a lot better for you! Super quick and super scrumptious.

PREPARATION **5 mins**   COOKING **None**   SETTING TIME **2 hrs**   MAKES **9**

50g	**coconut oil** – melted (plus more for greasing)
85g	**ground almonds**
85g	**activated sesame seeds**[1]
1 tsp	**vanilla extract**
1–2 tbsp	**rice syrup** to taste

Melt the coconut oil on a low heat in a medium pan.

Add all the other ingredients and mix well.

Press firmly into a lightly oiled tin lined with baking paper (I use a bread tin).

Leave in the fridge for a few hours to set, or put in the freezer for about 15 minutes.

Once set, cut into your desired shapes with a sharp knife, and store them in the fridge.

1   For notes on activating nuts and seeds, see page 13.

Sesame Sticks melt quite quickly in warmer weather, so I'll pop them in the freezer for a while if I'm heading out with snacks on a sunny day.

Experiment with adding a tablespoon of cacao powder or carob, and some spices.

Apricot Bars

Perfect for a high energy snack on the go, and a great alternative to all those over-priced 'health' bars, which can be packed with junk or high in sugar content.

PREPARATION **10 mins**   SOAKING **12 hrs**   SETTING TIME **2 hrs**   MAKES **10 bars**

½ cup/70g	**dried apricots** – unsulphured and pre-soaked[1]
¾ cup/105g	**activated cashew nuts**[2]
¼ cup/35g	**activated seeds**
1 tsp	**ground cinnamon**
2 tsp	**vanilla extract**
a smidge	**butter/coconut oil** for greasing
1–2 tbsp	**rice syrup** to taste
1 tbsp	**chia seeds** (optional)

Grind the nuts and seeds in a spice/coffee grinder or high powered blender until very fine.

Mix together with all the other ingredients in a bowl. Make sure the mixture isn't too wet – add some more dry nuts or seeds, or some ground almonds if necessary.

Press firmly onto an oiled tin lined with greaseproof paper (I use a bread tin).

Pop them in the fridge for a few hours to set. Alternatively, they can be cooked in the oven at 170°C for 30 minutes, but leave them to cool completely before carefully taking them out of the paper.

Store them in an airtight container in a cool place.

1   Soak the fruit in lots of warm water, overnight if possible or for at least half an hour.

2   For notes on activating nuts and seeds, see page 13.

Try experimenting with different combinations of nuts, fruit, and spices.
Just a word of caution: each bar contains approximately 1 apricot, so the natural sugar content is quite high.
Be careful how many you eat in one go.

Ginger Peeps

A quick, fun and easy one to do with the kids, little or big...

PREPARATION **15 mins**   MINIMUM RESTING **30 mins**   COOKING **8 mins**   MAKES **15 biscuits**

100g	**butter/coconut oil** – melted (plus more for greasing)
175g	**brown rice flour**
3 tbsp/65g	**rice syrup**
1 tsp	**baking powder**
1 ½ tsp	**psyllium husk powder**
2 tsp	**ground ginger**
2 tsp	**ground cinnamon**
2 tsp	**vanilla extract**
1 squeeze	**lemon juice**

Put all the ingredients in a big bowl, mix well and form into a ball.

On a floured surface, press the mixture to about 5mm thick. I use my hands as it's too wet for a rolling pin.

Press into biscuits using cutting shapes of your choice, and place on a baking tray using a fish slice.

Cover the mixture with a clean cloth and leave at room temperature to rest for 4 hours if you can, or at least 30 minutes (see page 5).

Set your oven to 170°C.

Cook in the oven for 8 minutes until slightly browning – check regularly as they overcook quickly.

Allow to cool for about 5 minutes before placing on a wire rack.

Store in an airtight container for up to a week.

Hobnots

Having succumbed to Hobnobs in the past, it was quite satisfying to come up with my own grain-free version. Packed with nutritious nuts and seeds and a gentle kick from the spices, the cinnamon also acts as a great blood sugar balancer.

PREPARATION **10 mins**   COOKING **12 mins**   MAKES **20 biscuits**

45g	**activated seeds**[1]
1 cup/100g	**desiccated coconut**
1 cup/100g	**ground almonds** plus extra for rolling
20g	**golden flax meal**
10g	**chia seeds** (or another 10g of the activated seeds above)
1 tsp	**psyllium husk powder**
2 tsp	**ground ginger**
1 tsp	**ground cinnamon**
1 tsp	**mixed spice**
a pinch	**salt**
30g	**rice syrup**
10g	**lucuma powder** (or another 10g rice syrup)
65g	**coconut oil** – melted (plus more for greasing)
1	**egg** (beaten)

Set your oven to 180°C.

Grind the seeds in a coffee/spice grinder if you have one, or just pop them in the blender for a few minutes. You want them quite fine but a little texture is OK and can add some nice crunch.

Add all the dry ingredients in a big bowl and mix well.

Add all of the wet ingredients and mix again until well combined, forming into a ball of dough.

Flour the surface with the ground almonds and press the mixture to about 4mm thick. Don't worry if it's a bit fragile.

Cut into circles with a round cutter, and place on a lightly greased baking tray using a fish slice.

Cook in the oven for about 12 minutes until lightly browning.

Allow to cool for about 10 minutes before placing on a wire rack.

Store in an airtight container for up to a week.

1   Choose from a mixture of: pumpkin, sunflower, and sesame. For notes on activating nuts and seeds, see page 13.

Flaxmeal can easily go rancid. It's best to buy whole golden linseed which should be stored in a dark place or the fridge, then grind what you need before you use it or do a week's worth and pop it in a jar in the fridge.

Lemon Cumin Biscuits

Cumin and lemon, a match made in heaven...

PREPARATION **10 mins**   MINIMUM RESTING **30 mins**   COOKING **10 mins**   MAKES **10**

1 tbsp	**cumin seeds**
125g	**butter/coconut oil** – melted (plus more for greasing)
50g	**rice syrup**
2	**lemons** – grated rind and juice
1 tsp	**vanilla extract**
1 pinch	**salt**
175g	**brown rice flour**

Dry fry the cumin seeds on a low heat turning often until browning (about 2 minutes), and set aside.

In a medium bowl, mix the cumin seeds, butter, syrup, lemon rind and juice, vanilla extract, and salt.

Work in the flour with a fork to make a ball.

Cover the mixture with a clean cloth and leave at room temperature to rest for a few hours, or at least 30 mins (see page 12).

Set your oven to 170°C.

On a floured surface, roll out the mixture to about 5mm thick.

Cut into biscuits using cutting shapes of your choice, and place on a baking tray using a fish slice.

Cook in the oven for 10 minutes until lightly browning.

Allow to cool for about 5–10 minutes before placing on a wire rack.

Store in an airtight container.

Fantastic Fats

Thankfully, the "low-fat" era seems to be coming to an end, with more and more people coming round to the idea of the importance of getting the right kinds of fats. Finally the mainstream seems to realise that butter is good for you! One thing to note, however, is that radiation levels are high in dairy produce, so it really is worth buying organic.

It almost goes without saying to steer well clear of trans or hydrogenated fats like margarine, due to their adverse health effects.

So what to use instead? The only oils I ever use for cooking are coconut oil, butter, and ghee. Olive oil should never be used for cooking as it becomes toxic once heated.

Choose butter that comes from grass-fed animals only. The best one I've found is called **Berkeley Farm Butter** (which I buy from Abel & Cole). Another decent option is **Vrai** (www.vrai.fr), which you can buy from larger health food stores and some bigger international food shops.

Coconut oil is a marvellous thing. Its health benefits include improving good cholesterol and lowering the bad, boosting metabolism, improving thyroid health, and increasing energy. To read more about this wonder oil see the book *Eat Fat, Lose Fat* by Mary Enig and Sally Fallon.

Coconut oil is worth buying organic if possible. It is often cheaper to buy it in bulk (see my Resources List, page 107). When I can't get a huge pot of it I go for **Biona's 'Coconut Oil Cuisine'**, which is a lot cheaper than all other organic coconut oil, and has been steamed so as to reduce some of the strong coconut taste, without losing any of its fantastic benefits.

Cakes & Bakes

Simple Sponge Cake

A more traditional type of cake except it doesn't have any flour (keep that quiet though, and no one will notice!). Good for birthday parties, and easily jazzed up, or make into fairy cakes instead.

PREPARATION **25 mins**   COOKING **40 mins**   MAKES **1 cake or 18 fairy cakes**

85g	**butter/coconut oil** – melted (plus more for greasing)
85g	**rice syrup**
1 cup/240ml	**coconut milk** or dairy-free milk
4	**eggs**
zest and juice of 1	**orange**
1 tsp	**vanilla extract**
180g	**ground almonds**
80g	**coconut flour**
1 tsp	**baking powder**
½ tsp	**bicarbonate of soda**
1 pinch	**salt**
15 drops	**food grade orange essential oil** (optional)

For the Icing

80g	**coconut oil**
2 tbsp/65g	**rice syrup**
10g	**lacuma powder** (or a little more rice syrup)

Set your oven to 180°C.

Add all the wet ingredients to a blender and mix well, setting aside a little of the orange zest.

Add all of the dry ingredients and mix again, or transfer to a large bowl if it doesn't fit.

Put the batter into a well-greased, round 20 cm cake tin lined with greaseproof paper.

Cook in the oven for about 40 minutes until a skewer comes out clean. I check after about 15 minutes, and if the top is browning I will cover it with foil.

Allow to cool for about 10 minutes before turning out onto a wire rack.

Leave the cake to cool completely before icing, (you can pop it in the fridge to speed this up).

To Make the Icing

Melt the coconut oil in a glass bowl over some hot water.

Add in all the other ingredients and mix well.

Pop the bowl in the freezer and set a timer for 3 minutes. It may take longer but take it out when about half of it has gone cloudy.

With an electric whisk, whip for a few minutes. It should get thicker until it becomes like a whipped butter consistency. If not, put it back in the freezer for a minute.

Spread it onto the cooled cake (if the cake isn't cool, it will melt the icing). This is easiest to do when the icing is at room temperature.

Sprinkle the remaining orange zest on the top, and some crushed pistachios if you are using them.

Store the cake in the fridge, where it can be kept for about a week.

Instead of using the orange, add 70g cacao powder with the dry ingredients and a few tablespoons into the icing to transform it into a chocolate cake. Or my favourite: 100g raw, activated pistachio nuts, 2 tsp of cardamom powder and ½ tsp of rose water to make a lovely pistachio and rose sponge.

Carrot Cake with Coconut Icing

This cake has such a lovely combination of spices and flavours. Don't be put off by the long ingredients list, this doesn't take long once you get the hang of it, and it's well worth the effort. This recipe also makes delicious muffins if you prefer.

PREPARATION **20 mins**   COOKING **45 mins**   MINIMUM RESTING **30 mins**   MAKES **1 cake**

210g	**carrots**
1 cup/125g	**activated walnuts**[1]
1 cup/160g	**pre-soaked dried fruit**[2]
432g tin	**pineapple** (in natural juice) – drained
	or the same weight of fresh pineapple
175g	**butter/coconut oil** - melted (plus more for greasing)
3	**eggs**
1 squeeze	**lemon juice**
50g	**rice syrup**
1½ cups/185g	**brown rice flour**
1 cup/100g	**desiccated coconut**
1½ tsp	**baking powder**
1 tsp	**psyllium husk powder**
2 tsp	**ground cinnamon**
2 tsp	**mixed spice**
1 tsp	**cardamom powder** (or any mixed spice)

For the Icing	
90g	**coconut oil**
60g	**rice syrup**
1 tbsp	**vanilla extract**
90g	**soft sheep or goats cheese**
a little	**raw chocolate or walnuts** to decorate (optional)

To Make the Cake

Mix the carrots in a blender until they are finely chopped. Add the walnuts and fruit and give them a quick buzz. Add the melted butter, eggs, lemon juice, and rice syrup, and whizz again.

Mix in all the dry ingredients by hand, or in the processor if you prefer a smoother texture.

Put the mixture in a big bowl, cover with a clean cloth, and leave for 3 hours at room temperature, or for at least 30 minutes.

Set your oven to 180°c. Line a rectangular 28 x 18 cm cake tin with greaseproof paper.

After resting, give it a good stir. Pour the mixture into the cake tin.

Cook in the oven for about 45–50 minutes until a skewer comes out clean (I usually check after about 15 minutes and when the top starts to brown I cover it with tin foil).

Allow to cool for about 10 minutes before turning out onto a wire rack. If the cake looks quite moist, leave it for about 3 hours before slicing and it will firm up.

Leave the cake to cool completely before icing.

To Make the Icing

Melt the coconut oil in a glass bowl over some hot water.

Add in all the other ingredients and mix well.

Pop the bowl in the freezer and set a timer for 3 minutes. It may take longer but take it out when about half of it has gone cloudy.

With an electric whisk, whip if for a few minutes. It should get thicker until it becomes like a whipped butter consistency. If not, put it back in the freezer for a minute.

Spread it onto the cooled cake with a knife (if the cake isn't cool, it will melt the icing). This is easiest to do when the icing is at room temperature.

Top with some finely grated raw chocolate or chopped walnuts.

Store the cake in the fridge.

1   For notes on activating nuts and seeds, see page 13.

2   Choose from: raisins, apricots or prunes, proportions to your taste. Soak the fruit in lots of warm water, overnight if possible or for at least half an hour, then rinse well.

Squashy Courgette Cakes

Smuggle vegetables into your cakes and some people might be none the wiser.

PREPARATION **15 mins**   COOKING **30 mins**   MAKES **12**

35g	**squash/carrot**
40g	**courgette**
60g	**butter/coconut oil** – melted (plus more for greasing)
1	**egg**
85g	**coconut milk**
75g	**rice syrup**
30g	**pre-soaked raisins**[1]
80g	**ground almonds**
80g	**desiccated coconut**
1 tsp	**bicarbonate of soda**
1 tsp	**baking powder**
1 tsp	**psyllium husk powder**
1 tsp	**ground cinnamon**
1 tsp	**mixed spice**
1 tsp	**ground cardamom** (or more of the other spices)
2 tsp	**vanilla extract**
a pinch	**salt**

Set your oven to 180°C.

Peel the squash and cut into medium-sized chunks. Steam for about 6 minutes or until fairly soft.

Cut the courgette into medium pieces, and put it in a blender along with the squash. Add the oil, egg, coconut milk and rice syrup, and blend until well combined.

Add the rest of the ingredients and mix well.

Pour into greased cupcake trays allowing a little room to rise (they don't rise much).

Cook in the oven for 30 minutes or until a skewer comes out clean.

Allow to cool for about 5–10 minutes before placing on a wire rack.

Store in an airtight container – they stay nice and moist for days.

1   Soak the fruit in lots of warm water, overnight if possible or for at least half an hour. Rinse well before use.

Fruity Flapjack Cakes

These are a healthier version of the traditional flapjack, good for giving you slow-release energy and perfect for snacking and lunchboxes.

PREPARATION **10 mins**   SOAKING **Overnight**   MINIMUM RESTING **30 mins**   COOKING **25 mins**   MAKES **1 cake**

1 cup/160g	**pre-soaked dried fruit**[1]
40g	**activated brazil nuts**[2]
150g	**butter/coconut oil** – melted (plus more for greasing)
1 cup/90g	**jumbo oats** – pre-soaked overnight and rinsed well
½ cup/80g	**brown rice flour**
½ cup/50g	**desiccated coconut**
½ cup/47g	**ground almonds**
1	**apple**
30g	**activated seeds**
2	**eggs** – beaten
2 tbsp/42g	**rice syrup**
1 tsp	**vanilla extract**
1 tsp	**baking powder**
2 tsp	**ground cinnamon**
1 squeeze	**lemon juice**

Roughly chop the dried fruit, apple and brazil nuts.

In a big saucepan melt the butter on a low heat.

Add all the ingredients to the pan and stir well.

Spread into a rectangular 28 x 18 cm baking tray, greased and lined with greaseproof paper, and smooth down firmly with the back of a big spoon.

Cover with a clean cloth and leave at room temperature to rest for 3 hours if you can, or at least 30 minutes (see page 5).

Set your oven to 180°C.

Cook in the oven for about 25 minutes or until lightly browning on the top.

Allow to cool for about 10 minutes before placing on a wire rack. Store in an airtight container.

1   Choose from: raisins, apricots or prunes, proportions to your taste. Soak the fruit in lots of warm water, overnight if possible or for at least half an hour.

2   For notes on activating nuts and seeds, see page 13.

Rocking Rock Cakes

These flour-free fairy cakes are full of flavour and stay moist for days.

PREPARATION **10 mins**   SOAKING **2 hrs**   COOKING **15 mins**   MAKES **12**

40g	**activated seeds**[1]
50g	**dried apricots** – unsulphured and pre-soaked[2]
110g	**butter/coconut oil** – melted (plus more for greasing)
2	**eggs**
50g	**rice syrup**
2 tsp	**vanilla extract**
90g	**desiccated coconut**
90g	**ground almonds**
20g	**lucuma powder** (or a little more rice syrup or vanilla)
2 tsp	**mixed spice**
2 tsp	**ground cinnamon**
1 tsp	**ground cardamom**
1 tsp	**baking powder**
1 tsp	**psyllium husk powder**
a pinch	**salt**

Set your oven to 180°C. Grind the seeds in a spice grinder or blender until fine and set aside.

Put the drained apricots, coconut oil, eggs, rice syrup, and vanilla into a blender and mix until smooth.

Add the remaining ingredients and mix again until well combined.

Pour into greased cupcake trays or muffin tins.

Cook in the oven for 15 minutes or until a skewer comes out clean.

Allow to cool for about 5 minutes before placing on a wire rack.

Store in an airtight container for 4–5 days.

1   Choose from a mixture of pumpkin, sunflower and linseed. For notes on activating nuts and seeds, see page 13.

2   Soak the fruit in lots of warm water, overnight if possible or for at least half an hour.

Cheeky Chocolate Cake

This fantastic chocolate cake is lighter than your standard one, and most people wouldn't guess that carrots are even an ingredient! Adapted from a recipe kindly shared with me by the nutritionist Rani Louise.

PREPARATION **10 mins**   COOKING **30 mins**   MAKES **1 cake**

300g	**carrots** – chopped into a few pieces
90g	**ground almonds**
90g	**butter/coconut oil** – melted (plus more for greasing)
225ml	**coconut milk**
6	**eggs**
60g	**raw honey** (or rice syrup)
20g	**molasses**
45g	**coconut flour**
40g	**raw cacao powder**
2 tsp	**baking powder**

For the Icing

70g	**coconut oil**
70g	**raw honey** (or rice syrup)
35g	**raw cacao powder**
small piece	**raw chocolate or cacoa nibs** to decorate

Set your oven to 190°C. Line the bottom and sides of a 20-inch cake tin with greaseproof paper.

Place the carrots in a blender until very fine.

Add all the other remaining ingredients and mix until well combined.

Pour the mixture into the cake tin.

Cook in the oven for about 30 minutes or until a skewer comes out clean.

Allow to cool for about 10 minutes before turning out onto a wire rack.

To Make the Icing

Melt the coconut oil in a glass bowl over some hot water.

Add in all the other ingredients and mix well.

Pop the bowl in the freezer and set a timer for 3 minutes. It may take longer but take it out when about half of it has gone cloudy.

With an electric whisk, whip for a few minutes. It should get thicker until it becomes like a whipped butter consistency. If not, put it back in the freezer for a minute.

Spread it onto the cooled cake (if the cake isn't cool, it will melt the icing). This is easiest to do when the icing is at room temperature.

Top with some finely grated raw chocolate.

Store the cake in the fridge.

Super Soft Scones

These scones are a great alternative to their flour counterparts, and they stay moist and fresh tasting for days.

PREPARATION **15 mins**   SOAKING **Overnight**   COOKING **20 mins**   MAKES **14 small scones**

2 ½ cups/250g	**ground almonds** plus some extra for rolling
½ tsp	**bicarbonate of soda**
1 generous pinch	**salt**
55g	**butter/coconut oil** – melted
2	**eggs**
2 tbsp/45g	**rice syrup**
½ cup/75g	**pre-soaked raisins**[1]
1 tsp	**psyllium husk powder**
1 tsp	**ground cinnamon**
1 tsp	**mixed spice**
2 tsp	**vanilla extract**

Set your oven to 180°C.

Mix the ground almonds, bicarbonate of soda and salt in a medium bowl.

Add all the other ingredients and mix until well combined and forms into a sticky ball.

Put the dough onto baking paper, dust both the dough and your hands with ground almonds, and press the mixture out flat. Fold in half, then in half again.

Now press the mixture out again to approximately ¾ inches thick, sprinkle with more ground almonds, and cut out with a cutter until all the dough is used.

Place scones on a greased baking tray and cook for 15–20 minutes until the tops are slightly browned (they don't rise much).

1   Soak the fruit in lots of warm water, overnight if possible or for at least half an hour. Rinse well before use.

Enjoy with butter, sugarfree jam, or just as they are. They store well in a cool place or the fridge in an airtight container for 4–5 days.

Many Milks & Dairy Dilemmas

There are many issues surrounding the consumption of dairy products. Goat produce has been shown on the whole to be more digestible to us than cow's dairy. A big issue is the pasteurisation and homogenisation processes, which are very damaging to the milk, and among other problems removes the good bacteria. Two thirds of the population actually lack the enzyme needed to break down lactose in milk. As for calcium myth, there are many other foods that are high in calcium and are also much more healthful than dairy milk.

Soya milk (and soya products generally) are also to be avoided. Despite being so often sold under the "heath food" bracket, the dangers of soya are thoroughly documented in scientific literature. These include high levels of phytic acid, which block the absorption of vitamins and minerals, and the plant oestrogens found in soy have a number of potentially serious adverse effects. Fermented soya products like tamari, miso and tempeh, however, don't have the same problematic issues as the processed soya products such as tofu and soya milk, and are indeed healthful foods.

Luckily, there are so many other types of wonderful milk that we can enjoy. Coconut milk is one of my favourites because of its unique fatty acids.

Other great milk alternatives are nut and grain milks. One word of caution though: with all these traditional milk alternatives, many of those sold in shops will have hidden nasties such as additives, sweeteners, and sunflower oils. Only go for whole coconut milk with minimal other ingredients. For nut and grain milks it is really hard to find healthful versions, so always read the labels. As is often the case, the best option is to make your own if you can.

"When you cook for yourself and make good foods, you have plenty of energy to cook from scratch."

Sally Fallon

How to Adapt Recipes

I am often adapting recipes to leave out the gluten and refined sugars, and generally find this is a lot easier than one might imagine. It takes a bit of experimenting, and each recipe or ingredient can produce very different results. I've put together some general guidelines that you might like to try. Some of my best creations have come from adapting recipes and getting creative!

Replacing Refined Sugar in Recipes

As a general guide, I substitute the sweet ingredients in the recipe with rice syrup (or alternatives listed in my notes about sugar, page 3), and reduce the quantity by a third. Liquid ingredients will also need to be reduced by a quarter. As previously mentioned, though more healthful than refined sugar, all these sweeteners are best used in moderation.

Speaking of sweeteners, a lot of the recipes in this book call for vanilla extract. Be careful when buying it as many extracts sneakily have added sugar. I got caught out with the Neilson Massey brand once; their organic extract sold in health food shops is free from sugar but the one in the supermarket isn't, much to my disappointment! Vanilla pods are a great (albeit pricey) option, as is vanilla powder.

Flour Power

Many of us have too much low-quality flour in our diets. If and when we eat flour, the best form is sourdough, due to its long period of fermentation. But if you don't have time to make everything using sourdough, there are many decent gluten-free flours to choose from. These include brown rice, millet, and hemp flour, plus grain-free flours such as coconut, buckwheat, nut meal, quinoa, and gram flour. They all have their distinctive tastes and textures, so it's worth experimenting.

Doves Farm make a few flour mixes which are widely available. Though they produce good results in terms of texture, they aren't quite as preferable nutritionally as the flours listed above.

Replacing Wheat Flour in Recipes

In terms of adapting recipes, I replace wheat flour with a gluten-free one weight-for-weight. Ground almonds, seeds, and desiccated coconut can also be added to reduce the grain content. Coconut flour is wonderful but it absorbs loads of moisture, so you will need to use about ¼ of the amount and add in some eggs.

One final thought: gluten-free baking can often have a different texture. If you don't expect it to come out too light and fluffy, then you won't be disappointed!

Replacing Milk in Recipes

I use lots of coconut, almond, rice or grain milk, and these often work just as well to replace recipes with cow's milk or cream, in the same quantities.

Happy experimenting!

"I'm an organic kind of guy. To paraphrase 'Fight Club', the food you eat, ends up eating you."

Jarod Kintz

Chocolates

Raw Chocolates

It really is super quick and simple to make lovely looking and tasting chocolate! Containing far more antioxidants than its processed counterpart, cacao is also the highest whole food source of magnesium.

A word of caution: raw cacao has strong stimulating qualities and can affect some people's sleep. If I have any beyond about 3pm I'm often awake half the night!

PREPARATION **10 mins**   COOKING **None**   COOLING **1 hr**   MAKES **40 small chocolates**

100g	**cacao butter**
25g	**cacao powder**
30g	**activated cashew nuts**[1]
35g	**rice syrup**
15g	**lucuma powder**
1 tsp	**vanilla extract**

Melt the cacao butter and oil in a double burner or in a glass bowl over a pan of just simmering water. Remove from the heat when it has almost melted.

Mix the remaining ingredients in a blender until combined.

Add any optional flavours if you are using them (see below) and mix again.

Transfer to a jug, and pour into your containers or moulds. You need to work quite quickly before it starts to harden.

Pop into the fridge to set for about 20–30 minutes depending on the size of your moulds, or put them in the freezer if you want them to set quicker.

If you're using flexible moulds, carefully stretch the mould out either side of the chocolate to loosen it before gently popping them out.

Keep the chocolates stored in the fridge on warmer days.

1   For notes on activating nuts and seeds, see page 13. Alternatively, you can use ground almonds. Although they are not raw, this can be a good option if you're not able to grind the nuts very fine.

Optional Flavour Combinations

Spices – my favourites are cardamom and cinnamon, which can be dry roasted on a gentle heat for a few minutes to improve the flavour.

Activated nuts and seeds (see page 13 – pistachio with cardamom work well together).

Dried fruit.

Organic essential oils – e.g. peppermint, lemon, lime, orange, or lavender. One drop can go a long way, so be cautious when experimenting. Non-organic oils can contain all sorts of nasties so I suggest using at least food grade.

Cacau nibs.

"Superfoods" and green powders – e.g. pollen, maca, goji berries, spirulina, or barley grass powder.

Raw extracts – these come in many wonderful flavours. They aren't cheap, but are highly concentrated so you only need a tiny bit.

Other Notes

I recommend using silicone chocolate moulds that are widely available.

Make sure you keep all equipment and moulds completely dry, as any small amount of water can mess things up.

Strictly speaking, for the chocolate to be raw, it mustn't be heated above 42°C. For some people this is important, but I don't worry so much about it.

Sometimes I like to swap some of the cacao butter for coconut oil. This adds even more nutrients, and makes the chocolate melt more easily.

Finally, raw chocolate is an amazing art (and science!). There are many wonderful ingredients, flavour combinations, and techniques that can be used. The chocolate recipes in this book are a very basic guideline to get you started. There are many great resources, books, and courses for anyone wishing to further the art.

White Chocolates

Can the Milkybar kid have his chocolate and eat it? Yes! White chocolate is my favourite, and I seem to be able to tolerate cacao butter better than cacao powder later in the day without being up all night. If you're in the mood for indulgence...

PREPARATION **10 mins**   COOKING **None**   COOLING **1 hr**   MAKES **32 small chocolates**

140g	**cacao butter**
50g	**ground activated cashew nuts**[1]
20g	**lucuma powder**
45g	**rice syrup**
2 tsp	**vanilla extract**
a pinch	**salt**

Melt the cacao butter and oil in a double burner or in a glass bowl over a pan of just simmering water. Remove from heat when the fat is almost melted.

Add the remaining ingredients and mix in a blender until combined.

Transfer into a jug and then, working quickly, pour into your chocolate moulds.

Place in the fridge to set, (usually takes about 20-30 minutes depending on the size of your moulds), or pop in the freezer if you can't wait that long.

If you're using a flexible mould, carefully stretch the mould out either side of the chocolate to loosen it before gently popping them out.

---

1   For notes on activating nuts and seeds, see page 13. Alternatively, you can use ground almonds. Although they are not raw, this can be a good option if you're not able to grind the nuts very fine.

White chocolate looks great when coloured. Some of my favourite ingredients to use for colouring are wheatgrass powder to make a vibrant green, raspberries, and blueberries. For extra flair, you could try some layering: pour one colour into the bottom of the mould and allow it to set before adding another layer; or splattering: put small blobs of chocolate in the moulds and set well before filling with another colour.

Choc-Free-Chocs

If you're anything like me and can't look at any raw chocolate after a certain time of day without being awake all night, here's an alternative. These are also great for kids when you don't want to stimulate them (any more!).

PREPARATION **10 mins**   COOKING **None**   COOLING **1 hr**   MAKES **18 chocolates**

100g	**coconut oil** – melted
30g	**ground activated cashew nuts** (or ground almonds)[1]
12g	**carob powder**
20g	**lucuma powder**
2–3 tsp	**vanilla extract to taste**
a pinch	**salt**

Pop all the ingredients into a bowl or blender and mix well. Pour into your desired moulds.

Place in the fridge until set (or the freezer to speed it up).

They need to be stored in the fridge or freezer and will melt quite quickly in warmer temperatures.

1   For notes on activating nuts and seeds, see page 13. Alternatively, you can use ground almonds. Although they are not raw, this can be a good option if you're not able to grind the nuts very fine.

They are quite bitter, so a little rice syrup can be used if you like a sweeter taste. If they are too plain for you, experiment and use some of the flavour suggestions listed for Raw Chocolate, page 51.

Serious Salt

Salt is a necessary and beautiful mineral, essential to life. We cannot live without it, and every cell in our body needs salt. But today's common table salt is a manufactured form of sodium laced with toxic chemicals, and it lacks most of the important elements of its natural counterpart.

I recommend using Himalayan crystal salt, because it's known to be one of the purest salts available and is uncontaminated with any toxins or pollutants. Another alternative would be unrefined sea salt. Again this is another area of considerable debate!

Suspect Additives

In terms of additives commonly used in gluten-free flour, I've moved away from baking with xanthan gum because it's a fairly indigestible carbohydrate (and can cause some people digestive issues). I suggest, alongside other food additives such as carrageenan and guar gum, it's best avoided altogether.

The best replacements I've found so far are psyllium husk powder, ground linseed and chia seeds, all of which contain significant nutrients. I default to using psyllium husk powder as it seems to be the most effective and the cheapest, (a huge bag of it from eBay costs about £11). Simply replace the same quantity as the amount of xanthan gum listed in the recipe.

Puddings & Ice Ceams

Apple & Berry Crumble

This is a take on my mum's lovely apple crumble, which was a family staple of ours when I was growing up. She always used lots of ground almonds in the topping. Perfect for colder, cosy nights, as well as using up any half-eaten apples (that regularly turn up around our house).

PREPARATION **10 mins**   COOKING **30 mins**   SERVES **6**

¾ cup/75g	**ground almonds**
¾ cup/120g	**brown rice flour**
½ cup/45g	**desiccated coconut**
50g	**butter/coconut oil** – softened
5	**apples** (about 550g)[1]
2 cups/220g	**raspberries** (or blueberries, or both)
1 tsp	**mixed spice**
1 tsp	**cardamom powder**
1 tsp	**ground cinnamon**

Set your oven to 180°C.

Cut the apples into slices (I tend not to peel mine but you can if you prefer).

Put them in a saucepan with a little water at the bottom and cook on a medium heat with the lid on for about 5 minutes or until soft but keeping their shape, making sure they don't burn.

Mix all of the dry ingredients together with the butter and rub the mixture until it's like large breadcrumbs.

Drain any excess water from the apples and combine with the berries in a deep dish (about 26 x 16 cm) and top with the crumble mixture.

Cook in the oven for about 30 minutes until the topping is lightly browned.

1   I tend to use eating apples as they are much sweeter than cooking apples.

Lovely served with dairy-free custard, goats yogurt, or homemade ice cream. If I'm in a hurry, I just have mine with whatever milk is to hand.

Pancakes

Very quick and versatile, makes a lovely weekend breakfast treat. I like to make a big batch and have them on tap for days in a row.

PREPARATION **5 mins**   MINIMUM RESTING **30 mins**   COOKING **5 mins**   MAKES **8**

60g	**brown rice flour** (or buckwheat flour)
90ml	**coconut milk** (or another dairy-free milk)
30ml	**filtered water**
1	**egg**
1 tsp	**psyllium husk powder** (or bicarbonate of soda)
½ tsp	**apple cider vinegar** (or lemon juice)
1 chunk	**butter/coconut oil** – for frying

Add all the ingredients to a large jar, pop on the lid and shake well.

Take off the lid, and leave to stand covered with a clean cloth at room temperature to rest overnight if you can, or at least 30 minutes (see page 12).

Before cooking, stir or shake again.

Heat some butter in a pan until hot and quickly pour in enough mixture to cover the bottom (I like mine quite thin).

Cook for a few minutes on each side until nicely browning.

The mixture can be stored in the jar in the fridge with the lid on. It lasts for up to 5 days. Just shake well before each use. Lovely served with rice syrup and lemon, or some berries. They also make great savoury meals, we like to stuff them with scrambled eggs and spinach or smoked salmon.

Chia Pudding

Don't be fooled by their humble size, chia seeds are powerhouses of nutrition and are packed with nutrients. They are high in protein, healthy omega-3 oils and can help balance blood sugar. When soaked, they make great tapioca-like puddings.

PREPARATION **5 mins**   COOKING **None**   MINIMUM RESTING **3 hrs**   SERVES **2**

240ml/1 cup	**coconut milk**
30g/¼ cup	**ground activated cashew nuts**[1]
3 tbsp	**chia seeds**
1 tbsp	**rice syrup** (or lacuma powder)
½ tsp	**ground cinnamon**
1 tbsp	**vanilla extract**
a sprinkling	**cacao nibs** (optional)

Place all ingredients, except the cacao nibs, in a large mixing bowl or blender.

Mix everything together until well combined and smooth.

Pour into pots or glasses, and sprinkle with the cacao nibs if using.

Chill in the fridge for at least 3 hours, or overnight if you can, giving them a stir after 30 minutes.

1   For notes on activating nuts and seeds, see page 13.

Lovely topped with fresh berries and/or lightly toasted desiccated coconut. Add spices, nuts, seeds, or superfoods like maca or bee pollen, if you fancy.

Moreish Mousse

A great way to knock up a super quick pudding, and a nice alternative to sugar-filled chocolate yogurts or Angel Delight (I can't believe that's still around!).

PREPARATION **5 mins**   COOKING **None**   SERVES **2**

2	**medium avocados** (ripe)
1 tbsp/15g	**carob powder**
¼ cup	**coconut milk** (or other dairy-free milk)
1 tsp	**honey** (or rice syrup)
1 tsp	**vanilla extract**
a little	**lime zest** (optional)

Chuck it all in the blender and whizz up.

Pour into bowls or pots, topping with some grated lime zest if desired, and enjoy!

If you want to jazz it up you could add some ground nuts and/or spices. For a chocolate version replace the carob with cacao powder.

Spicy Orange Tart

A quick and simple more-ish treat that makes the whole house smell divine.

SOAKING TIME **overnight**   PREPARATION TIME **10 minutes**   COOKING TIME **35 minutes**   COOLING TIME **3 hours**

100g	**ground almonds**
4	**oatcakes** (about 40g)
80g	**butter/coconut oil**
20g	**rice syrup**
1 tsp	**mixed spice**
1 tsp	**ground cinnamon**

For the Topping

2	**eggs**
1 ¼ cup/275ml	**coconut milk**
90g	**rice syrup**
zest & juice of 1	**orange**
2 tsp	**ground cardamom**
80g	**coconut oil**
15 drops	**food grade orange oil**
a pinch	**salt**
1 small handful	**pecan nuts** - to garnish[1]

Preheat your oven to 180°C.

Grind the oatcakes in a blender until fine.

Add the remaining base ingredients and mix well.

Spoon about half the mixture into a lightly greased and lined 20 cm spring form tin, pressing firmly to cover the base.

Setting aside a little of the orange zest, add all the topping ingredients to the blender and mix well.

Pour over the prepared base and bake until golden (30–35 minutes).

Cool in the pan to room temperature on a wire rack (about 3 hours).

Garnish with the remaining zest and pecan nuts.

Gently remove from the pan and store in the fridge.

1   For notes on activating nuts and seeds, see page 13.

"All of the ways of preparing grains, nuts and other foods in traditional cultures actually increases the nutrients. Whereas the way we prepare our breads, vegetables and everything else often decreases them."

Sally Fallon

Lime Cheesecake

Yes, you can enjoy cheesecake without the dairy overload! This recipe is irresistibly creamy and delicious. The flavours of lime and coconut transport me to a tropical island. Even though it's made from healthy ingredients, it's still high in calories, so just bear that in mind when you reach for a second slice...

PREPARATION **20 mins**   FREEZING **6 hrs**   MAKES **1 cheesecake**

140g	**ground almond, pecan or hazelnuts**[1]
40g	**coconut oil** – melted
30g	**desiccated coconut**
1 tsp	**ground cinnamon**
1 tsp	**ground cardamom** (or mixed spice)

For the Filling

2 ¼ cups/250g	**activated cashew nuts**
1 cup/225ml	**unsweetened coconut milk**
80g	**coconut oil**
¼ cup/85g	**rice syrup** (to taste)
2 tsp	**vanilla extract**
zest & juice of 2	**limes**

1   If I'm in a hurry I will use a packet of ground almonds, but ideally activated nuts are best. For notes on activating nuts, see page 13.

Line a sprung cake tin with baking paper and lightly grease. For sweet individual cakes, make them in muffin trays by lining the bottom of the trays with some baking paper, and cut two strips of paper about 2 cm thick. Slip the strips down either side of the filling and when they are set gently pull on them for super easy removal.

Dry fry the desiccated coconut and spices for about 2-3 minutes on a medium heat.

Put them and the other base ingredients into the blender and mix well.

Press the base mixture very firmly into the tin with your fingers.

Put this in the freezer for about 30 minutes or until firm.

In the blender, add all the filling ingredients, except for a little lime zest, and mix well.

Pour the filling mixture onto the base, garnish with the remaining zest, and put it back in the freezer until hardened. This should take about 4-6 hours.

Leave it at room temperature for 10-15 minutes before serving.

Stores in the freezer for up to 2 weeks.

Chai Scream

I confess to being an ice cream addict, and I love chai, so for me this is a marriage made in heaven. I sneaked some squash in too and nobody seemed to notice.

PREPARATION **5 mins**   FREEZING **6 hrs**   SERVES **4**

160g	**butternut squash**
400ml	**coconut milk**
70g/½ cup	**activated cashew nuts**[1]
40g	**rice syrup**
1	**egg** (optional)
2 tsp	**vanilla extract**
1 tsp	**ground cinnamon** or mixed spice
1 tsp	**ground cardamom** (or more of the spices above)

Peel the squash and cut into medium-sized chunks.

Steam for about 6 mins or until fairly soft.

Grind the cashew nuts to a fine flour in a spice grinder or high-power blender.

Add all the ingredients to a blender and mix until well combined.

If you have an ice cream maker, pour in the mixture following your machine's instructions.

Otherwise, pour the mixture into a shallow container with a lid and freeze for about 6 hours or until fully set. Churn by hand every 2 hours or so.

Before serving, soften at room temperature for about 20–30 minutes.

1   For notes on activating nuts and seeds, see page 13.

Great for hot summer days. I freeze some in small pots for the kids, (well mainly for me actually) and take it out fully frozen, then an hour or so later they are ready to eat. Avoid that ice cream van if you can!

Pistachio Ice Cream

A summer treat, this has to be my favourite ice cream. It's so quick and simple. An ice cream maker isn't essential, though it tastes even more divine if you use one.

PREPARATION **5 mins**   FREEZING **8 hrs**   SERVES **3**

400ml	**coconut milk**
80g	**activated raw pistachio nuts**[1]
1	**egg**
2 tbsp/45g	**rice syrup**
2 tsp	**ground cardamom**
1 pinch	**salt**

Put the nuts in the blender and very lightly mix until you have chopped the nuts into chunks.

Add all the remaining ingredients and mix until well combined.

If you have an ice cream maker, pour in the mixture following your machine's instructions.

Otherwise, pour the mixture into a shallow container with a lid and freeze for about 8 hours or until fully set. Churn by hand every 2 hours or so.

Before serving, soften at room temperature for about 20–30 minutes.

1   For notes on activating nuts and seeds, see page 13.

Instant Ice Cream

You really can make ice cream in minutes on a hot summer's day.

PREPARATION **5 mins**   FREEZING **None**   SERVES **1–4!**

2 parts	**frozen mixed berries**
1 part	**coconut milk or goat's yogurt**
	rice syrup to taste

Just mix it all up in the blender – voila!

Get creative and add vanilla extract, lacuma powder, nuts or nut butter, carob powder, your favourite spices... The possibilities are endless!

The Organic Minefield

If money and time were no option, I'd buy only the most seasonal, local, and organic produce I could lay my hands on. Alas many of us have very full lives, and I'm always trying to find ways in which my "compromises" can be knowledgeable and informed.

Something I found really helpful is a wonderful resource by The Environmental Working Group called '**The Shoppers Guide to Pesticides in Produce**' (www.ewg.org/foodnews). This is a list of 50 products ranging from the ones containing the most pesticides to the ones with the least (they do free printable versions which you can stick on the fridge).

At the top of the "Dirty Dozen" for 2016 are strawberries, apples, and nectarines, and topping the "Clean Fifteen" list are avocados, sweetcorn, and pineapples.

So if, like me, you aren't always able to buy all organic, it's worth checking to see which ones you are able to "get away with", so to speak.

Cheesy Hearts

This is a nice simple recipe for cheese straws that have transformed into tasty hearts, but choose whatever shape you fancy and they might even leave you with a cheesy grin on your face... For a little kick, try adding a pinch of cayenne pepper, smoked paprika, or dried herbs.

PREPARATION 20 mins   MINIMUM RESTING **30 mins**   MAKES **18 biscuits**

180g	**brown rice flour**
90g	**butter/coconut oil** – softened
150g	**organic feta cheese**
1	**egg**
1 splash	**apple cider vinegar**

Put the flour in a large bowl and rub the butter in well until it's like breadcrumbs.

Add all the other ingredients and mix until you have a ball of dough (it can be done in a blender, but make sure you only pulse it very briefly otherwise it goes too mushy). If it's too dry, add a little water.

On a floured surface, roll out to about 5mm thick.

Cut with shaped cutters or make into straws and place on a baking tray.

Cover the tray with a clean cloth and leave at room temperature to rest for 30 minutes or up to 8 hours (see page 12).

Set your oven to 180°C.

Cook in the oven for about 12 minutes until lightly browning, checking after 10 minutes.

Allow to cool for about 10 minutes before placing on a wire rack.

They are best eaten on the day they're made, but can be stored in an airtight container in the fridge for up to 3 days.

Easy Gluten-Free Bread

There's nothing quite like the smell of fresh bread wafting around the house and the butter melting into it when it's still warm. If you're going for gluten-free bread this is by far superior to most shop-bought varieties that are often laden with additives and sugar.

PREPARATION **10 mins**   MINIMUM RESTING **30 mins**   RISING TIME **90 mins**   COOKING TIME **75 mins**

400g	**brown rice flour**[1]
100g	**gram flour**
500 ml	**warm water**
a splash	**apple cider vinegar or a squeeze of lemon juice**
40g	**coconut oil / butter – melted**
2 tsp	**quick yeast**
2 tsp	**psyllium husk powder**
1 tsp	**salt**

Mix the flour, water and vinegar in a big bowl. Cover with a clean cloth and leave at room temperature for 24 hours if you can, or a minimum of 30 minutes (see page 12).

Use some of the melted oil to grease a bread tin, making sure it is covered well.

Add the rest of the oil to the flour mixture along with the remaining ingredients and mix thoroughly.

Pour the mixture (it will be fairly runny) into the bread tin, cover with a cloth, and leave to rise in a warm place for 90 minutes.

Put in the oven and cook at 200°C for 10 minutes, then turn temperature down to 180°C and cook for a further 65 minutes. When it's done it should sound hollow when tapped.

Take it out of the tin and leave to cool for at least an hour or so before slicing.

Store in a cool dark place (but not in the fridge). It freezes well, just slice it first.

---

1   Or another gluten-free flour/s of your choice. Sometimes I add some buckwheat flour. For a grain-free version you could use a mix of buckwheat and gram flour.

Try adding crushed coriander seeds and molasses, herbs, activated nuts or seeds.

The Liberated Loaf

This savoury loaf is packed with vitamins and minerals, and is great for anyone wanting to avoid flour or yeast. High in protein and fibre, quick to make, and it makes great toast. It may not be the cheapest loaf, but it is filling so you don't need much, and it freezes well if by any chance you don't devour it all in a few days.

PREPARATION **10 mins**   MINIMUM RESTING **2 hours**   COOKING **1 hour**   COOLING TIME **3 hours**

1 ½ cups/150g	**ground almonds**
1 ½ cups/150g	**desiccated coconut**
1 cup/130g	**activated pumpkin seeds**[1]
1 cup/140g	**activated sunflower seeds**
½ cup/90g	**flax meal**
½ cup/65g	**activated hazelnuts**
3 tbsp	**psyllium husk powder**
2 tbsp	**chia seeds**
1 tsp	**salt**
¼ cup/55g	**butter/coconut oil**
2 ½ cups/590ml	**water**

1   For notes on activating nuts and seeds, see page 13.

Flaxmeal can easily go rancid. It's best to buy whole golden linseed which should be stored in a dark place or the fridge, then grind what you need before you use it, or do a week's worth and pop it in a jar in the fridge.

In a big bowl, add together all the dry ingredients and stir well.

In a medium saucepan, melt the coconut oil, then add the water and whisk until well combined.

Add this liquid to the dry ingredients and stir well.

Place into a well-greased 2lb loaf tin lined with greaseproof paper, smoothing out the top with the back of a spoon.

Cover the mixture with a clean cloth and leave at room temperature to rest for 2–4 hours (see page 12). It will become firmer as the liquid gets absorbed by the husk powder and flaxseed.

Set your oven to 170°C. Bake your loaf for about an hour. It should sound hollow when tapped.

Allow to cool for about 10 minutes before carefully turning out onto a wire rack.

It is important to let it cool completely before slicing.

Store in a sealed container at room temperature for up to 5 days. It freezes well too – best to slice it first so you can pull out just what you need.

Quick Pizza Bases

A simple, quick recipe for a great alternative to this wheat based staple. The same recipe also makes good burger buns.

PREPARATION **10 mins**   MINIMUM RESTING **30 mins**   COOKING **30 mins**   MAKES **2 bases or 5 burger baps**

225g	**brown rice flour**
2 pinches	**salt**
1 tsp	**quick yeast**
1 tsp	**psyllium husk powder**
40g	**butter/coconut oil** (plus more for greasing)
160ml	**coconut milk** (or dairy-free milk)
1 splash	**apple cider vinegar or lemon juice**
1	**egg**

In a large bowl, mix together the flour, salt, yeast, and psyllium husk powder until well combined.

In a medium saucepan, melt the coconut oil, then add the milk and heat until it's just warm. Mix thoroughly.

Add this liquid to the dry ingredients along with the egg and vinegar.

Stir well and form into a soft ball of dough.

Cover the mixture with a clean cloth and leave at room temperature to rest for 30 minutes or up to 4 hours (see page 12).

Divide the dough into two, and on a floured surface roll out to about 5 mm thick.

Place on an oiled baking tray and leave to prove for about 30 minutes.

Set your oven to 180°C.

Cook in the oven for about 10 minutes, then apply your choice of pizza topping, return to the oven, and cook for about 20 minutes or until the crust is golden brown.

I like to avoid the nightshade family, so instead of a tomato base, I use pesto sauce, pureed beetroot or other pureed vegetables such as sweet potato, carrot, or parsnip.

To Make Burger Buns

Roll the dough into a long sausage shape and cut into 5 equal pieces. Form these into rounds.

Place on an oiled baking tray and leave to prove for about 45 minutes.

Set your oven to 180°C.

Cook in the oven for about 30 minutes, or until a light golden brown.

They are lovely eaten warm. If there's any left store them in a cool dark place.

Spelt Sourdough Bread

This is my all-time favourite loaf of bread. Sourdough is a naturally fermented dough without manufactured yeast and is nutritionally superior to any other type of bread.

People have made bread this way for thousands of years, and it really is easy and quick to make once you're in the swing of it, as well as immensely satisfying. The sourdough process is richer in bio-available minerals than quick-rise bread, and also lower on the glycaemic index. It liberates the minerals in the flour and creates an abundance of folate and B vitamins.

If made with a long fermentation process like in this recipe, the bacteria digests the gluten that is present in the flour. Even when using a modern day wheat flour, one Italian study by Rizzello C et al, in 2007, showed that the gluten content in the sourdough bread had reduced to 12 parts per million, compared with 75,000 parts (fewer than 20 parts per million is considered to be gluten-free).

As with raw chocolate (page 43), it is an enormous subject to be explored. This recipe will get you started, and is the one I use at home to make our daily bread. As there are so many variables in terms of temperature and humidity (you are after all working with a living thing), I have found it a real learning journey which I still get wrong from time to time! It's worth persevering though, and there are many resources out there for support.

I have chosen spelt for this recipe, but rye and kamut flour are also worth exploring. Spelt is an ancient cereal grain and a distant cousin to wheat. It is higher in protein and minerals than most modern day wheat flour. Always use wholemeal spelt flour.

Spelt Sourdough Bread (continued)

There are two stages to making a sourdough loaf. First the 'starter' (think of it as yeast), then the loaf itself, which needs to rest overnight before finishing and baking.

To Make the Starter

PREPARATION **5 days** at 3 mins per day

	Days 1–4 each
25g	**wholemeal spelt flour**
50g	**warm water** – about 40°C

Day 1

Mix the flour and water into a sloppy paste in a medium bowl.

Cover with a clean cloth and leave overnight in a warm place.

Day 2, 3 and 4

Measure out a new batch of flour and water, and stir into the mixture from the previous day.

Cover with the cloth and return to a warm place overnight. It may show signs of frothing, and have a grey-ish liquid on the top.

Day 5

You should now have a sourdough that smells fruity and has bubbled up. It should taste mildly acidic, which is fine and how it's meant to be.

Storing the Starter

The starter can be left at room temperature for a few days. After that store it in the fridge, where it will keep for a couple of weeks, or indefinitely given weekly flour and water feeds.

If you think you can't use it in that time, I suggest either giving some away, or storing it in the freezer. Yeasts do lose some viability in the freezer, so if possible it's best avoiding it, but using a frozen sourdough is still much quicker than starting from scratch.

It is a good idea to refresh the starter immediately before freezing, by adding one day's quantity of flour and water, and to refresh again when it comes out in the same way. It's also worth feeding it the day before you bake if it's been in the fridge for a while. I store mine in a glass jar with the lid slightly loose so that it's not airtight.

To Make the Bread

PREPARATION **2 days** at 4–5 mins per day   COOKING **75 mins**   MINIMUM RESTING **1 day**   MAKES **1 loaf**

	Day 1
150g	**wholemeal spelt flour**
100g	**sourdough starter**
200ml	**warm water**

	Day 2
360g	**wholemeal spelt flour**
200ml	**warm water**
5g	**salt**
a little	**butter/coconut oil** – for greasing

Day 1

In a big bowl, stir together the flour, sourdough starter, and warm water.

Cover with a clean cloth and leave overnight in a warm place for 12–24 hours.

Day 2

Add the remaining flour, 190 ml water, and the salt, to the mixture from the previous day.

Stir together well for about a minute to form a slightly wet dough.

Pour into a well-greased bread tin, cover with a cloth, and leave for a further 2–3 hours – avoid really warm places at this stage.

Set your oven to 220°C.

Cook the loaf in the oven for 10 minutes, then reduce the temperature to 180°C and cook for a further 65 minutes.

Turn out onto a wire rack, and leave to cool and rest for several hours, ideally 12 hours.

Store in a paper bag or a bread bin. The loaf usually lasts about 4–5 days at room temperature. It freezes well, but slice it first so you can just pull out what you need from the freezer as you go.

I like to add 5 tbsp of crushed coriander seeds on Day 2 at the final stage before baking, and sprinkle some on top as well.

Many-Seed Thins

Savoury, seedy, herby, and yummy crackers.

PREPARATION **15 mins**   COOKING **15 mins**   MAKES **26**

1	**egg**
10g	**coconut oil** – melted (plus extra for greasing)
½ cup/50g	**ground almonds**
½ cup/65g	**activated nuts**[1]
1 tbsp/7g	**coconut flour**
¼ cup/35g	**activated pumpkin seeds**
2 tbsp/30g	**sunflower seeds**
2 tbsp/20g	**chia seeds or sesame seeds**
2 tbsp/13g	**hemp seeds**
1 tbsp/5g	**golden flax meal**
2 tsp/2g	**dried herbs of your choice**, e.g. oregano and thyme
½ tsp/3g	**salt**

Set your oven to 170°C.

In a medium bowl, whisk the egg and coconut oil until frothy and set aside.

Pulse the ground almonds, nuts, and coconut flour in a blender until well ground.

Add in the seeds, flax meal, herbs, and salt, and pulse until almost fully ground (leaving a little texture makes a nice crunch).

Add in the coconut oil and egg, and pulse until a dough ball forms in the blender (or transfer to a bowl to do this).

Cut out 2 large sheets of greaseproof paper.

Place the dough in between the two sheets of paper and gently roll it out to a thickness of 3–4 mm (it's important to get them nice and thin).

Cut to your preferred size – I use a 7 cm x 4 cm rectangular cutter – and using a fish slice, gently transfer onto a large greased baking tray.

Bake in the oven for about 15 minutes.

Allow them to cool to room temperature on the baking tray before serving.

Store in an airtight container for up to 7 days.

1   Choose from walnuts, brazils, or cashew nuts. For notes on activating nuts and seeds, see page 13.

If you want them crispier, they can now be put in a dehydrator on about 70°C for 12 hours.

Delicious with savoury dips or some sheeps/goats cheese.

Flax meal can easily go rancid. It's best to buy golden linseed which should be stored in a dark place or the fridge.
Then grind what you need before you use it, or do a weeks worth and pop it in a jar in the fridge.

Smoky Paprika Thins

These were adapted from a cracker recipe, but my tasting panel insisted they didn't "crack" enough, hence their title. Easy to make, and a good replacement for oatcakes, which often contain sunflower oils or heated olive oil, which I try to avoid.

PREPARATION **10 mins**   COOKING **15 mins**   MAKES **24**

1	**egg**
1½ cups/150g	**ground almonds**
¼ cup/36g	**sesame seeds**
¼ cup/40g	**golden flax meal**
1 tbsp/14g	**butter/coconut oil** – melted (plus more for greasing)
2 tsp	**smoked paprika**
½ tsp	**salt**

Set your oven to 170°C.

In a large bowl, whisk the egg until frothy.

Add in all the remaining ingredients, mix and combine into a dough ball.

Cut out 2 large sheets of greaseproof paper.

Place the dough in between the two sheets of paper and gently roll it out to a thickness of 3–4 mm (it's important to get them nice and thin).

Cut to your preferred size – I use a 7 cm x 4 cm rectangular cutter, and using a fish slice, gently transfer onto a large greased baking tray.

Bake in the oven for about 15 minutes.

Allow them to cool to room temperature on the baking tray before serving.

Store in an airtight container for up to 7 days.

Please take a look at the notes on Many-Seed Thins (page 81) which also apply.

Fruity Cautions

Some people who cut down on refined sugar end up consuming large amounts of fruit or fruit juice. When we drink fruit juice, especially the ones from concentrate, we are taking in all the sugars from the fruit but none of the fibre, which is fundamental in helping us to process all the sugar.

This elevates our blood sugar more rapidly than eating the whole fruit; the same can be said for most fruit smoothies. A glass of apple juice contains about four apples – a lot more than we would usually eat in one sitting!

Watch out for dried fruit too. It has most of the water removed, concentrating the sugars. Half a cup of fresh cranberries contains 2 g of sugar, whereas the same quantity of dried cranberries contains a whopping 37 g (9 teaspoons). A handful of dried fruit does the same thing to our blood sugar as a Mars Bar!

Some tropical fruit, like kiwi, does have nutritional value, but I think it's worth avoiding most tropical fruit, such as bananas, mangos, figs, and dates, due to their very high sugar content. One date is over 60% sugar – check out how many "healthy" snacks have dates as a main ingredient!

Often dried fruit also means preservatives, such as sulphites. These can cause nasty respiratory problems and digestive issues, and kids especially don't tolerate them well. We also need to watch for polyunsaturated oils, such as vegetable and sunflower oil, that are often added to dried fruit to stop them sticking together. These bad fats are unstable and can easily turn rancid.

Drinks

Almond & Hazelnut Milk

A great alternative to dairy, almond milk has more calcium than cow's milk, and is high in magnesium, energy, proteins, and lipids, and has an alkalizing effect on your blood. My homemade nut milk was always very watery, and I missed the creamy texture of the not-so-healthy shop versions. Then I discovered a trick which makes it thicker, and which made me a very happy bunny.

PREPARATION **10 mins**   MAKES **3 glasses**

1 cup/120g	**activated blanched almonds**[1]
¼ cup/35g	**activated hazelnuts**
6	**dried apricots** – unsulphured & pre-soaked, or vanilla extract to taste
1 pinch	**salt**
5 cups	**filtered water** – use less for a creamier texture

Place all ingredients in a blender and mix until smooth.

Strain through a fine mesh sieve, or unbleached muslin over a regular sieve. Scrape the last creamiest bits with a spoon or give the fabric a good squeeze.

Add the milk to a large saucepan on a high heat.

Stir constantly until it reaches a high temperature but not boiling. Just before it reaches a boil, the hot liquid will go from watery to slightly creamy as you stir.

Immediately remove from the heat at this point.

Pour into a glass jar or pitcher and allow the mixture to cool in the refrigerator before serving.

It will keep for at least 4 days in the fridge. Shake or stir before serving.

1   For notes on activating nuts and seeds, see page 13.

We love to use the leftover nutty pulp for baking, adding to smoothies, curries, crumbles, or putting on porridge. You can try substituting some or all of the almonds for brazil nuts, cashew nuts, or hemp seeds.

Charming Chai

For me, not much beats the smell of freshly made chai wafting around the house. It's traditionally made with black tea, but I prefer a caffeine-free version using rooibos. I find it such a comforting drink and it always reminds me of being in a field at a great festival.

PREPARATION **20 mins**   MAKES **3 cups**

1 ½ cups	**dairy-free milk** of your choice
1 ½ cups	**filtered water**
2	**rooibos teabags**
2	**cinnamon sticks**
6	**cardamom pods**
1 tsp	**cloves**
1 inch	**fresh ginger** – skin on and roughly sliced
10	**black peppercorns**

Roughly crush all the spices and ginger with a pestle and mortar.

Bring the water to the boil in a saucepan and then add all the spices and ginger.

Simmer gently for about 10–15 minutes (or anything up to an hour if you wish).

Add the teabags and simmer for another 4–5 minutes.

Add the milk and heat through without boiling.

Strain into a jug and serve nice and hot.

It keeps well in the fridge for 3–4 days.

I have also been known to chuck everything in at the beginning (while the traditionalists turn in their graves!).

Coconut Milk

Coconuts are highly nutritious and packed with beneficial medium chain fatty acids and lauric acid, alongside many other vitamins and minerals. You can avoid the chemicals in the canned variety by making your own. It really is quick, easy, and far cheaper than any shop bought version.

PREPARATION **5 mins**   MAKES **4 glasses**

1 ½ cups	**desiccated coconut**
4 cups	**filtered water**
1 tsp	**vanilla extract** (optional)

Boil the water then leave it to sit for a few minutes to cool.

Put the coconut in a blender and add the water.

Blend on high for several minutes until it begins to thicken.

Rest for a minute and mix again for a minute.

Strain through a fine mesh sieve, or unbleached muslin over a regular sieve.

To make sure you get the last creamiest bits out, use a spoon to scrape the sieve at the end, or give the cloth a really good squeeze.

Add the vanilla extract if you're using it.

Drink immediately or store in the fridge with a lid on, where it lasts for about 4 days.

The leftover pulp can be dried in a low oven or dehydrator, and used in place of desiccated coconut. The cream of this milk will separate into a solid block when it's stored in the fridge just return it to room temperature where it will soften enough to be stirred in.

Merry Berry Smoothie

A quick and easy way of getting your veggies without even realising it.

PREPARATION **5 mins**   MAKES **2 glasses**

1 handful	**kale**
1 cup	**berries** – choose from blueberries, blackberries, or raspberries
2 cups/420ml	**coconut milk** (or dairy-free milk)
1 tsp	**vanilla extract**
2 tbsp	**lacuma powder** – or honey/rice syrup to taste

Add the milk, water, and kale to the blender and mix until smooth.

Add the rest of the ingredients and mix again.

Pour into glasses and enjoy!

Silky Smoothie

Smoothies have become increasingly popular, but not all smoothies are created equal! Avoid flooding your bloodstream with insulin by keeping the fruit to one variety, and however tempting it is to chuck in a load of bananas, stick to ripe avocados or berries so as to avoid the big sugar hit. Less is more as they say. This smoothie is packed with goodness, takes minutes to make, and is easily adapted.

PREPARATION **5 mins**   MAKES **2 glasses**

1	ripe avocado
2 cups/480ml	coconut milk (or grain-free milk)
1 small handful	ground cashew nuts
1 tbsp	ground seeds – choose from chia seeds, flaxseeds or hemp seeds
1 tsp	cinnamon powder
1 tsp	super greens powder such as barley grass, wheatgrass or spirulina
1 tbsp	lucuma powder – or honey/rice syrup to taste

Add all the ingredients to a blender and mix until well combined.

Pour into glasses and enjoy!

FareShare Charity

I wanted to donate some of the profits from this book to charity, and when I came across FareShare in Brighton it seemed like an obvious choice. A percentage of every book sold will be going to them, and here's a bit more about what they do:

FareShare Sussex fights food poverty by redistributing quality surplus food from the food industry to organisations working with homeless and vulnerable people in the community. The organisations they deliver to support a wide range of vulnerable people, including rough sleepers, women and families escaping abuse, people recovering from addictions, people who suffer from HIV/AIDS, teenagers and adults with learning difficulties, isolated older people, and young children from deprived areas. The food they supply reaches over 5000 people every week, dramatically improving access to healthy food for the most disadvantaged people in our society.

Not only do they reduce waste and tackle food poverty, FareShare Sussex also aim to improve people's life chances through their volunteer programme. They work with volunteers who have struggled with addiction, homelessness or been through the penal system, to offer them a structured environment to develop employment skills, social skills and reintegrate with society.

www.fairesharesussex.org.uk

FareShare Sussex is a charitable project run by registered charity City Gate Community Projects, charity number 1093245.

Links & Resources

NUTRITION

www.stevenacuff.com
Steven's website has a really useful online forum with loads of useful information, and includes recommended and avoid food lists and menu planners.

www.connectwithnutrition.co.uk
Kirsten Chick, nutritionist and lecturer, who, among other things, runs fantastic courses, workshops and retreats.

www.ranilouise.com
Rani Louise is another great nutritionist who kindly donated the chocolate cake recipe on page 40.

STOCKISTS

www.tree-harvest.com
Suppliers of a huge range of natural products. Great for bulk orders, public or trade accounts available, this is my favourite place to get raw chocolate supplies and superfood powders.

www.vrai.fr
Fantastic French butter

www.paynesbeefarm.co.uk
Payne's Bee Farm

www.rawhealth.uk.com
Raw Health (suppliers of raw honey)

www.naturaldispensary.co.uk
Suppliers of high quality supplements, many great brands all on one website

GENERAL REFERENCE

www.westonaprice.org
A non-profit charity spreading the research of nutritional pioneer Dr Weston A Price

www.nourishedkitchen.com
Reviving healthful traditional foods

Wild Fermentation: The Flavour, Nutrition, and Craft of Live-Culture Foods
by Sandor Ellix Katz

Nourishing Traditions
by Sally Fallon

Eat Fat, Lose Fat
by Mary Enig and Sally Fallon

Cellular Awakening: How Your Body Holds and Creates Lights
by Barbara Wren

OTHER STUFF

www.faresharesussex.org.uk
FareShare Charity

www.wellbeing-centre.org
UK's first integrated NHS Health Centre

References

Jarod Kintz, *A Story That Talks About Talking Is Like Chatter To Chattering Teeth, And Every Set of Dentures Can Attest To The Fact That No...* (Universe Publishing, 2007)

Maria Rodale, *Organic Manifesto*, (Pennsylvania: Rodale Press, 2010)

Thich Nhat Hanh, *Peace Is Every Step*, (London: Random House, 1991)

www.healthyfoodforliving.com/public/180print.cfm

www.kitchenstewardship.com/2010/03/04/real-food-face-off-nourishing-traditions-vs-nourishing-days

About the Author

Jo trained as a dancer and went on to perform extensively and teach people of all ages. When a chronic pain issue that arose in adolescence made it difficult to continue pushing her body so hard, she turned to practising yoga, which she taught for eleven years. Juggling the demands of her young son and four stepchildren eventually led her to step down from teaching and focus more on an ever-increasing passion for food. She now enjoys sharing that with family and the wider community in Brighton where she lives.

Find out more about Jo and Joy Food Revolution at www.joyfoodrevolution.com

Index

Lightning Source UK Ltd.
Milton Keynes UK
UKOW07f1104250816

R1536400001B/R15364PG281379UKX1B/1/P

9 781781 325216